WE NEED YOUR PURPOSE
#ThisIsHowWeChangeTheWorld

TEVIN BLIGNAUT

WE NEED YOUR PURPOSE

#ThisIsHowWeChangeTheWorld

PART 1

Printed in the Republic of South Africa

First Printing, 2020

978-0-620-86669-9 (print)
978-0-620-86670-5 (e-book)

Published by Tevinthespeaker (PTY) LTD

"Let us empower you"

13 Albida Place, Eagle View

Breaunanda, 1724

www.Tevinthespeaker.co.za

Table of Contents

WE NEED YOUR PURPOSE

#ThisIsHowWeChangeTheWorld

Presented by

"LET US EMPOWER YOU"

DEDICATION

To my wife and son, you are my greatest work.

To my parents, thank you – for everything.

To those who contributed to this project, shalom.

To those who have read it, Baraka Allahu fiik (May God's blessings be upon you).

To the owner of purpose, may your will be done on earth as it is in heaven.

ACKNOWLEDGEMENTS

This project has been the amalgamation of many minds. Thank you to all who have contributed. Every conversation, meeting, email, Whatsapp message, and phone calls have contributed to the final product of this book. Thank you for all the love and support. It is truly appreciated and forever cherished.

May this book and the contribution of your work be impactful across the many nations of the world.

INTRODUCTION

I hope that after reading this book and considering its information your life will begin to reflect its true potential. A potential that displays the dominion nature that has been reserved for you since the beginning of time.

Dr. Myles Munroe wrote a book on the topic of releasing your potential. It is here, where he describes the graveyard to be the richest place on earth as there lie ideas, strategies, and solutions that have never come to life because there lay people who were too busy pursuing a life outside of their purpose. What a tragedy to think that so many people, who had amazing thoughts and concepts which had the potential to bring positive change in the world, died with all of it inside of them. This report cannot be the same for our generation and even more so, the generations to follow.

And so, began the search for answers. I have found something a truth that has been around since the beginning of time – a treasure chest filled with precious jewels. This treasure is priceless, it holds a value that no amount of monetary could ever equate to it. It is so powerful that it can set you free from the life you have been living. A life where you were made to feel less than anything you are truly meant to be. This treasure has the power to restore you to a place of dominion and rulership. It can bring you wealth without toiling for it; it can give you hope in the most challenging circumstances, and it can give you the power to control your life again. This treasure lies in understanding the concept of purpose.

I would like for you, as the reader, to understand that I have done extensive research concerning this topic and have applied its truth to my own life and the results have been nothing short of miraculous. I have also been able to discuss this concept amongst friends and their lives have been transformed as well. Therefore, I am certain, that once you understand the concept of purpose and apply it in your life there will be evidence of its fruitfulness.

Therefore, I have written a two-part book series concerning this topic and I encourage you to study them both. May your life be transformed by the concept of purpose – may you live the life you always dreamed of and may you accomplish all that was meant for you.

CHAPTER ONE

THE POWER OF PRINCIPLES

To fully grasp the concept of purpose, there must be a clear understanding of the nature and power of principles. According to Dictionary.com the term principle has two definitions.

The first definition states that principles are a fundamental truth - meaning they are of central importance and must be followed very closely if the desired outcome is to be met. The second definition states that principles are generalized laws that apply across various spaces – meaning that the same principles which are applied in one space can also be successfully applied in another. In other words, principles are the master-keys of life and once you discover them, they can be used on all doors you may desire opening.

Think back to your days in school, during mathematics class, you were never told to study numbers to find the correct answers because they change all the time. Instead, you were told to study the formulae (principles) because these would give you access to the correct answer. And just like in school, if you don't know the correct formula you are most likely going to get the wrong answer.

The secret path to success

Every person on this planet wants to be successful. The problem is that most people do not know the correct principles (formulae) that will result in that success and so, they experiment with a trial and error mentality and the result is usually chaos, anxiety, depression, and unfulfillment. But if people were to discover the correct principles and apply them where necessary the result would be a success because success is predictable. Thus, the design of this book.

I have done the research and have found the common principles for success that have been used by generations of people. People who have changed the world, accumulated great wealth and established world-renowned brands such as Andrew Carnegie who had brought the steel trade to the USA. Henry Ford who had established the Ford brand. Colonel Harland Sanders who established the KFC brand.

Dr. Myles Munroe who established Munroe Global Incorporated. Oprah Winfrey who is a legendary talk show host. Novak Djokovic and Serena Williams, who are recognized as two of the greatest tennis players in history.

Barack Obama who became the first African American president of the United States of America. Nelson Mandela the receiver of the Noble Peace Prize and Trevor Noah, who is a world-renowned comedian and many others.

These are people who have impacted the world, and they did it by simply understanding and then applying the principles shared in this book. The principles are as follows:

1.   Vision

2.   Desire

3.   Faith

4.   Decisions

5.   The gift

6.   Mastermind

7.   The subconscious mind

8.   The brain

9.   The Spirit

These are the principles that when applied will guarantee success. This book will discuss each of these concepts so that you may take them and apply them in your own life – that you too may become successful because with success comes power and with power, we can change the world.

May you, re-discover the power of your purpose.

CHAPTER TWO

THE POWER OF VISION

In the context of this book, vision does not refer to sight but rather what you see beyond your current disposition. It's the active use of your imagination which supersedes the involvement of your five senses, which means that you can have a vision for your life that is beyond your current circumstances or life experiences. For example, you can have a vision of your dream home whilst you are still broke or living with your parents. Or you can have a vision of your million-dollar business whilst you are still working for someone else. To put it plainly, vision is the future you hope to live in.

The power behind this principle is this; whatever you envision for your life can be pulled into a tangible reality. That is why it is so important to have a vision for all the spaces in your life including your career, marriage and relationships etc.

A vision gives you something to look forward to

This principle is so powerful because it dictates the plan for your life and gives you something to look forward to in the future. It also allows you to plan and strategize now for who you hope to become. This is vital to understand because the decisions you choose to make today will impact the vision you have for your life.

Your vision will dictate what you do and with whom you do it. For example, when I discovered this principle, I envisioned myself as a published author. So naturally, I had started researching the industry to find out what it takes to become a best seller. I also started engaging with other authors and attended meetings just to learn more about the space and because of that, I was able to connect with likeminded people and build new relationships that have already added much to my life.

Vision protects your life

Vision will protect your life because it will keep you – should you choose to commit to it – from people who are going nowhere in their lives. Please note this, those who are going nowhere in their lives will always want you to go there with them. But vision will separate the people and things that add no value to who you are and where you are going.

Vision gives life to the body

Another secret behind the power of vision is that it gives you energy. Colonel Harland Sanders founded the brand of KFC at the age of 65. That's incredible because so many people have retired by then, but he saw something in his future that gave him new life and so, he worked to make the vision become reality. And it did, it became so successful that his brand is recognized and well known in over 100 countries worldwide. What is the vision for your life?

CHAPTER THREE

THE PRINCIPLE OF DESIRE

Desires pull you into action

The principle of desire is a crucial step in the journey toward success because it has the potential to pull you into action. In other words, it will bring you to do something about the vision you see in your head.

Desire is wanting to succeed as bad as you want to breathe

To desire, something means to deeply want or even crave it, to the point where it is all you think about and it consumes you entirely. Dr. Eric Thomas explains this principle best, when he speaks about the story of the young man, and the guru. The story goes like this; a young man asked his guru to show him how to become successful and the first lesson he was taught was the principle of desire.

To prove the point, the guru took the young man to a beach, where they got into the water until they were chest-deep when suddenly, the guru dipped the young man and kept him underwater for as long as he could. When the young man finally freed himself to come up for air, the Guru explained that success must be desired as much as breathing. Only then would he become successful.

The principle of desire is necessary because it will pull you into action and out of your comfort zone – where nothing significant ever happens

I remember when I discovered this principle and how it impacted my life. I had started my own company working as a strength and conditioning coach for private clients. It was during this time where I discovered my gift of speaking and teaching – and this is all I desired to do. The desire grew to the extent where the business at the time became a burden to me because it was taking me away from my true passion. I also remember the many conversations with my wife regarding this growing passion and dilemma I was faced with.

We spoke at lengths about how much we needed the income from the business to pay for the house, levies and electricity bills but the desire I had overpowered these circumstantial needs and so, we sold all our possessions to pursue this desire and we have never looked back since. Both the car and house were sold and that afforded us the time and freedom to work on our passions which produced

this book series and so many other success stories.

The principle for desire is important to understand

because it is much more than a simple want. A want can be

described as wishful thinking, but a desire becomes an

obligation because it will bother you until you do something

about it.

CHAPTER FOUR

THE PRINCIPLE OF FAITH

Have faith

The word faith has nothing to do with religion, it simply means your capacity or ability to believe in something or someone. Therefore, I challenge you, to have faith in yourself and your abilities. Have faith that all things are working out for your good. And finally, have faith that everything you need, when you need it will become available to you. This is one of the most effective tools anyone has available to them and it works wonders. I have seen miracles happen because of this principle.

Let me give you an example, I have been working on the second edition of this book series for almost a year now. And finally, I thought the work had been completed and I needed an editor to help compile the final product. I therefore met with the editor, discussed and agreed upon the amount for services. The challenge I was presented with however, was that I didn't have any money because at this point I had already quit my training business to focus on speaking and I had no idea where the funds would come from but I had faith. And as it does, faith proved to be true. Almost immediately, I was contacted with the opportunity to work with the Zambian national football team and the agreed wages not only covered the editorial expenses for the book but so much more. This is the power of faith.

Anything authentic must be tested

Whenever you have a vision or idea that you believe is worth pursuing, you will always see it as the final product, where nothing is missing, and there is nothing broken. Faith is then necessary to believe in that final product whilst you are going through the wilderness.

The wilderness is a sub principle of faith and the process of refinement where your vision and idea will be pushed to its breaking point, but this is not to destroy you, it is to make you better. Think of the process of a diamond, it undergoes several steps of refinement and extreme pressure to prove its authenticity and value.

Step one is to search and find the diamond thereafter, the drawing and marking phase begins. This process involves marking the surface area of the diamond, after which the rock is cut and broken down so that the diamond may be fully exposed.

Step two refers to the cleaving and sawing phase; here the diamond will be split from the remaining pieces of the rock using a laser or sawing apparatus to help remove all impurities that have tried to attach itself to the diamond.

Step three and four are known as the brut and polishing phase; here the diamond is shaped by a laser beam and then polished to give its beautiful, bright and shiny appearance that we see in eloquent jewelry pieces today.

This four-step process of the diamond is the wilderness. The process is never meant to destroy you, it's for your benefit and the development of your faith. It will make you stronger and prepare you for the next challenge life throws at you.

The secret to overcoming the wilderness

The secret to overcoming the wilderness is changing your perspective on it. To put it another way, you should fall in love with the wilderness process because it exposes your true value and power to succeed in life. There is an age old saying, God will never give you what you cannot endure. So, the very fact that a challenge has been given to you – no matter how devastating it may be - is proof that you are able to overcome it. The people who do not understand this truth will tend to give up whilst they are in the midst of the wilderness. But this should not be the case with you because you have this information.

The wilderness is your place of growth and refinement

Think of a gymnasium, when someone decides they want to improve their muscular strength, they must begin to lift heavier weights – if not, they will remain the same or worse, lose the muscle mass they have already gained. This is the truth about the wilderness.

CHAPTER FIVE

THE POWER OF DECISIONS

Your life is the sum of decisions you made

Your life, as it is right now, is the sum of decisions that you have made. That is why this principle is important to understand because it instantly gives you the power to change things. So, if you are not happy with the life you have been living, change your decisions and your life will begin to move towards a different light.

When I discovered this principle, I immediately stopped doing the things that brought me so much stress. Suddenly, I became free, because I was no longer bound by the bad decisions that I have been making; the decisions that have kept me captive for so many years. For example, before I discovered the concept of purpose that lead me to these principles, I had little control over my life.

I was working as a general manager for a small-sized company and of course, I was overworked and severely underpaid. I worked overtime most days of the week which meant I would only get home around 7.30 in the evening. During the workday I would be responsible for incoming and outgoing calls; incoming and outgoing emails, team meetings, hiring employees – which included the interview process and dismissal process. I was also responsible for team marketing strategies, media and public relations for our events, event coordination, business and relationship development, television interviews and so much more. But worst of all, I became the personal driver for the owner of the company. I remember on many occasions when I was called to the offices just to take him for grocery shopping -

this is truly unbelievable now that I look back at this

experience.

And what's crazy is this; I couldn't understand why

this was happening to me. But now that I have discovered

the principle of decisions and I understand its power, I could

see how much of this terrible experience was my own doing.

I had surrendered control over my life because I had hoped

this job would be my ticket to success. And so, I made

decisions that kept me aligned with my hopes at the time

which was to earn large sums of money and it nearly

destroyed me.

Understand this, bad decisions can destroy your

potential and purpose. So, make good decisions.

The secret to making decisions

The secret to making decisions is simple - and again this secret can be applied to any decision you need to make now or in the future - always consider the consequences, because if you can accept the consequences, the decision becomes easy. Therefore, I challenge you, make decisions that will benefit your future and the vision you see for yourself. Choose the consequences that you give you, life and life more abundantly.

CHAPTER SIX

THE POWER OF YOUR GIFT

Specialized knowledge

Specialized knowledge is a strange topic because it does not necessarily refer to your level of education or your certification. It does, however, focus on the knowledge of your gift which must be refined by education. Therefore, for the context of this book, education refers to acquiring knowledge for a specific skill set that you may have.

In other words, there is something that you naturally do better than others with the least amount of effort – this is your gift. And this is the thing that you need to be refining because your gift is the tool that will make room for you.

Many people have gone to university to study a degree so that they could get a job and become wealthy. But many of these people end up sad, stressed, depressed and with no wealth to give evidence of their knowledge. The problem is universities cannot give people their gift because it's something they are born with and it is your responsibility to discover it and use it in the world.

Your gift will make you famous

Once you have discovered your gift and you refine it, it will make you famous. Think of any celebrity in any space and note what they are famous for – they are famous for simply expressing their refined gift. Trevor Noah was born in South Africa and he discovered his gift to tell stories and make people laugh. He went on to refine this gift and now he is known all around the world as one of the best comedians. Lionel Messi was born in Argentina and he discovered his gift to play football. He refined it and now he is known as one of the greatest players to ever have played the game. Gordon Ramsay was born in Scotland and he discovered his gift of cooking. He refined it and is now known as one of the world's greatest chefs.

To put it another way, there is nothing is missing from who you are, compared to those who have become successful, they have simply discovered their gift and refined it to bring them success. You are capable of the same.

CHAPTER SEVEN

THE PRINCIPLE OF THE MASTERMIND

The mastermind is one of the greatest secrets to wealth and prosperity. The principle is founded on the idea of a group of people coming together to purposefully discuss solutions to a concept.

The Power of friends

The mastermind is by far the most effective way of learning and developing because it's a discussion with your group of friends. In this space, you can extract information from people who have different experiences and expertise that can add great value to your concept.

For example, the idea to self-publish this book was based on the recommendation of my mastermind. I gave them a few chapters to read and they were impressed by it. I was also encouraged by the mastermind to complete the work and they held me accountable with the many follow up meetings, messages, and phone calls.

You are also more likely to get honest opinions regarding your ideas and that's important because it can shift your thinking and highlight gaps that you never saw before. For example, the format of the YouTube series available on @Tevinthespeaker has changed much since the beginning and that is because of the discussions I had with the mastermind. The initial concept I had was to create videos with pictures being used to visually describe the message of the voice. However, the mastermind felt the format of the

presentation was missing the connection that I hoped for and then they suggested the possible solutions to improve the channel - and it worked. The presentation format changed from pictures to short video clips, until finally recording the message as myself.

The mastermind can be your source

The mastermind principle is so powerful that it can bring you to accomplish in one year, what many people never achieve in their lifetime because they choose to strive for their success alone. A secret in life is this, we can always do more and be more - together. We are not meant to compete as though life is a race to success where only those who come first will get the prize. We must help as many

people as we possibly can.

That's the basis for this principle. Everyone in your

mastermind is gifted and talented in some-way or the other.

All you need to do is find a way to leverage off that gift so

that it not only benefits you but also them.

Let's look at the mastermind alliance between

Tiffany Haddish and comedy mogul Kevin Hart. The two

actors collaborated and worked together on a movie called

Night School – which grossed over 28 million dollars over

the first three days of its release. The mastermind alliance

between these two actors was formed when Kevin Hart saw

a live stand-up comedy performance by Tiffany Haddish.

The two of them connected after the show in the parking lot

where he discovered that she was living in her car. At the

end of the night, he gave her 300 dollars to check herself

into a hotel for the week and he also gave her the task of writing down the vision and goals for her life. One of which included being a famous actor.

This powerful demonstration of the mastermind resulted in increased income and perpetual loyalty for both actors. It also allowed Tiffany Haddish to learn from Kevin Hart who had experience in the industry she wanted to impact. Your mastermind alliance can do the same for you.

CHAPTER EIGHT

THE SUBCONCIOUS MIND

AND THE BRAIN

The subconscious mind is powerful because it dictates how the conscious will behave

The power of the subconscious is that it acts as your storage facility and a processor which leads to outward actions. To put it another way, everything that you have ever heard, seen, read, felt or experienced has all been stored in your subconscious mind. So, whatever has been stored will determine how the conscious mind responds when a similar experience or occasion arises. This means that, the subconscious mind is the processor that determines how you will respond to any given situation.

Think of when you drive a car: the act of driving is your conscious mind because it's outward, but how well you drive will be determined by the subconscious because you might have felt good about driving and so your confidence is high and that makes the driving experience more pleasant for you. If you did not have a good experience or something negative happened whilst you were driving, it will impact on how well your conscious mind operates the car. And this is the secret to becoming more effective at anything, change the subconscious mind. Repeat in your mind what you want the subconscious to believe and it will become your actual thought.

For example, I have started many businesses in my lifetime and most of them failed. My first failed business was in sports development for young kids and to raise funds for the company I would host football tournaments. The problem was I lacked marketing and administrative skills, so only five or six teams would participate, and they would complain because the event always started later than scheduled. Another failed business was my bootcamp idea. This was a strange one because it looked to be going well. I added two trainers to my team who were perfect for the roles but unfortunately it never worked out because I misused and misplaced the funds that were meant to pay them. To make it up to my trainers, I offered them shares in the business but then I became distracted with my job and completely disappeared.

Now, to many people that would have steered them off course so that they never try it again, but in my subconscious, I have purposed to view those failures and stepping-stones toward my success and that gives me the confidence and belief to try again.

The Power to forgive

The same principle can apply to your relationships. For example, to forgive someone who has betrayed your trust, you need to replace the offensive memory with a memory that focuses on the good of that person. Let that be the memory that you focus on and your outward response to that person will be different. This means that the secret to forgiving is not in the heart but in the mind.

The Power of the human brain

The human brain is the most powerful tool on the planet. Everything that we get to experience in life today is a result of the human brain. Cars, houses, trains, airplanes, computer technology, the internet, and artificial intelligence are all the result of the human brain.

Study to show yourself approved

The human brain is so powerful that it can master anything. And the secret to its mastery is to study. The principle, study to show yourself approved has been a truth since the beginning of time. Whatever you choose to study, you can own that information so that it becomes yours to use. My study of the principles I am writing about, to the point of understanding, has afforded me the ability to propel my life through the process of active application. Because of this, I have transitioned from being a victim of unemployment to becoming a business owner, business consultant, an activist for peace across the world, author, motivational speaker and teacher on the topics of purpose and the kingdom mandate.

CHAPTER NINE

THE POWER OF THE SPIRIT

The spirit connects you back to the source

The human being is made of three main components which are body, mind, and spirit. Think of it this way, the body is the suit that keeps the spirit legally here on earth. The mind is the mechanism by which the spirit produces thoughts and actions. And the spirit gives life to both of these components' because it is the connection back to your source who is God.

You cannot operate without your source

It is impossible to operate without your source. Let me prove it. The source of any fish is the water. If you remove the fish from the water (source) it will die. It is the same for new technology. The source of a laptop is the charger. If you remove the charger from the laptop it will die – it may work for a few hours but eventually, it will die.

It is the same for the human race, the spirit is the connection back to our source who is God. And the more we rely on the spirit, the more we can begin to think and operate like God. That is why it is so important that you connect and engage with the spirit because the spirit holds the truth about your purpose.

The spirit is consistent

Many people in the world believe they can operate without the spirit and the result is chaos. This is because people who depend on the mind and body to achieve their success becomes susceptible to its flaws. For example, the mind can be influenced by negative thoughts and emotions, and the body can be influenced by disease and sickness.

But when you operate by the spirit who is consistent and never changing, the flaws of the mind and body can be overridden. For example, my wife was diagnosed with cancer in the uterus. This disease has killed many people with great potential but my wife who operates by the spirit was able to overcome it. The doctors instructed her to take the tablets that would kill the cancer in the uterus for the next three to four months and then she would be re-examined to find out what the next steps would be. But during this time, my wife discovered the concept of purpose and she had faith in it. She reasoned that for her purpose to be true, she had to overcome the sickness and live, so that she could use it to benefit the world. The rate of her healing completely shocked the doctors to the point where they could not understand how it happened, but the truth is this, she simply reconnected back to the source. The source is the river of life and it flows endlessly.

CHAPTER TEN

THE POWER OF YOUR PURPOSE

There is nothing in this world without a purpose

The principle of purpose is a universal concept which means it applies to everything and also everyone. The definition thereof is the reason for which something exists and that means you too were born for something. You have a purpose attached to your life and it is your responsibility to discover what it is and live by it to the best of your ability.

Purpose can only demand from that which is already present

Purpose can only demand from that which is already present and that means you were born with everything that you need to be successful in this life. Therefore, the discovery of your purpose guarantees success.

Let me explain, the previous chapters of this book discussed the principles of success that every great person in history went on to discover and apply in their life. The application of these principles not only resulted in success but a global impact and when you, discover the concept of purpose, you will realize that all these principles are already built-in you. Think of a product manufacturer; the manufacturer can only demand that the product performs the functions that it has been designed to.

The same concept applies in the corporate space. The manager can only demand that the person performs the functions necessary for the role they are employed in nothing else. And to ensure the person fulfills the functions of that role, the manager will need to supply the employee with all the necessary information to succeed. It is the same with you.

The power of purpose

Once you have discovered the concept of purpose and you understand it, your life will begin to change, because suddenly, you realize how much power you truly have. This happened to me when I discovered the concept of purpose. I no longer needed to be employed because I understood that the power to succeed is not in people or things, it's in my ability to cultivate who I truly am. This same discovery happened to many of the people in my mastermind.

Let me tell you a story, a good friend of mine discovered his gift in the architectural space. He worked for a few companies and there he designed buildings that ranged from residential houses to estate homes and even large university campuses. He too discovered the concept of purpose, and soon after, he quit his job to start his own company in property development. He began presenting his business ideas to CEOs of large companies and now, they are looking to partner with him. The business concept is to create wealth on a mass scale that allows people from impoverished backgrounds to invest in property.

The same thing happened to my wife. When she discovered the concept of purpose, she no longer applied for jobs instead she began cultivating her gift of cooking.

She now believes, that through food all diseases in the world can be cured. This is the ultimate secret to success: to become the best version of you, but you can only

know that by discovering, understanding and cultivating the

concept of purpose.

CONCLUSION

This book forms part one of the series, #ThisIsHowWeChangeTheWorld.

The time has come for peace on the earth. Peace can be established when the power to succeed has been restored to everyone from all walks of life. The challenge was that the keys to success have been hidden but now it has been rediscovered through the concept of purpose. Once you discover this concept and understand it, it will expose the undeniable truth that you are a solution to the problems of the world and your purpose is to solve them. This is how we bring peace to our world and that is why we need your purpose.

REFERENCES

1 Dr. Myles Munroe, Releasing Your Potential

2 https://www.dictionary.com/browse/principle

3 Napoleon Hill, Think & Grow Rich

4   https://www.biography.com/business-figure/colonel-harland-sanders

5   https://believersportal.com/biography-dr-myles-munroe/

6   https://www.biography.com/media-figure/oprah-winfrey

7   https://www.biography.com/athlete/novak-djokovic

8   https://www.biography.com/athlete/serena-williams

9   https://www.biography.com/us-president/barack-obama

10   https://www.sahistory.org.za/people/nelson-rolihlahla-mandela

11 https://www.trevornoah.com/about/

12   https://www.biography.com/business-figure/colonel-harland-sanders

13   https://www.youtube.com/watch?v=-raYgOmYPvQ

14 https://www.dictionary.com/browse/faith

15 https://www.dictionary.com/browse/education

16 https://www.trevornoah.com/about

17 https://www.biography.com/athlete/lionel-messi

18   https://www.biography.com/personality/gordon-ramsay

19

https://www.youtube.com/playlist?list=PL0QcAaAn

z0oUdXNt41kyj_zQTUrThvaMA

20 https://hiddenremote.com/2018/09/30/box-office-night-school/

21

https://www.spiritualresearchfoundation.org/about-us/fundamental-articles/what-are-human-beings-body-mind-soul/

ABOUT THE AUTHOR

Tevin Blignaut is an internationally recognized strength and conditioning coach, motivational speaker, lecturer, author, and business consultant. He is a firm believer in the precepts of purpose and the Kingdom mandate which is to bring Heaven on earth. Thus, bringing peace, prosperity and wealth to everyone across the world from all walks of life.

He is the founder of Tevinthespeaker (PTY) LTD which specializes in several services such as motivational speaking, teaching the principles of success, creative arts and music, book publishing and business consultations.

Tevin Blignaut has earned multiple degrees from the University of Johannesburg and various other certificates from internationally recognized establishments.

Additional copies of this book and other book titles published by TEVINTHESPEAKER (PTY) LTD is available on our website: www.tevinthespeaker.co.za

WE ARE COMMITTED TO IMPACTING THE WORLD. ARE YOU?

PLEASE CONNECT WITH US ON

SOCIAL MEDIA: